Integrating the Feminine Spirit

Returning to the Womb of Creation

By

Sam Oliver

ISBN: 1-4107-3724-1 (e-book)
ISBN: 1-4107-3725-X (Paperback)

Library of Congress Control Number: 2003092144

This book is printed on acid free paper.

Printed in the United States of America
Bloomington, IN

1stBooks - rev. 05/05/03

Dedication

I am dedicating this book to:

My Mom

Acknowledgments

I want to thank my Hospice patients and families who continue to inspire me to do what I do at Hospice as a Spiritual Counselor. Dying patients have taught me much about living in soul. This book is about healing through the feminine side of the soul. My Hospice patients have taught me this in many ways.

Most of all, I want to thank God for the opportunity to put in words some of my deepest longings to know a kind of love that transcends the conditions of our world.

Table of Contents

Book Review

Roberta Reynolds Spencer, Director of Support Services

(The Center for Hospice and Palliative Care, Inc. in South Bend, IN)

Sam Oliver's timely focus on the feminine is well suited for today's world. Individuals seeking hope, healing, peace and compassion, qualities often associated with the feminine, will find this book useful and rewarding. While the title may appear most attractive to women readers, it is equally valuable for men seeking a better understanding of the feminine side of nature and the way these qualities are presented in all of us, male or female.

The author asks the reader to draw within to a "womb like" state reflective of contemplation. It is here that his writing helps us to understand the heart, and reveals the soul which is unconditional love. The challenge in this progression is to better understand and appreciate the self through an awakening to the feminine spirit that leads to contentment and centeredness.

Integration is one of the book's themes. Throughout the book Oliver talks of the importance of integrating the feminine and masculine, heart and soul, human and divine, fullness and emptiness, and birth and death. He asks readers to answer for themselves the question, "do we struggle or dance with these challenges?"

Incorporating his own poetry to summarize the chapter's content, Oliver invites readers to use their own creativity to reflect and pose questions about the true meaning of "integrating the feminine sprit" in the personal notes page provided at the end of each chapter. Allowing the feminine spirit to be our guide offers us an opportunity to see the world with an inner depth, to see the soul and respond. Sam Oliver provides us a meaningful reflection on how to commence this journey.

Book Review

Valarie Pompey, MS, CHPN, APRN, BC

(The Clinical Coordinator @ The Center for Hospice and Palliative Care, Inc. in South Bend, IN)

Sam Oliver, through observation, personal reflection and poetry, shares his own experience of personal discovery. He guides the reader along a path of enlightenment towards finding the feminine spirit. This book gives us permission to slow down, take a deep breath and focus inward. Insightful and soulfully written, those who are drawn to read this book will soon discover that the simplest joys and true peace is not found with worldly gain, but is found within us. The feminine spirit is that innate aspect buried deep within our being. Allowing this part of ourselves to flow forth, we sway and dance effortlessly to the rhythmic drums of life instead of struggling through it.

For all who seek meaning and purpose, for those seeking to quench what seems to be unquenchable thirst, upon reading the final pages of this book comes a realization that it is the pains of our feminine self-repressed but fully developed, like a fetus in a mother's womb-waiting to be born that we are feeling.

By following the path developed by Reverend Oliver, one can soon awaken and bring forth a renewed sense of self. With this rebirth, if you will, comes a new appreciation for those that we ever so briefly encounter as well as those held close to our hearts.

May blessings come to those who read this book as to its author.

Forward

(Kathleen Singh, author of, *The Grace in Dying: How we transform when we die*)

It is an axiom in individual psychology that what is repressed will return to be heard and to be integrated. What is repressed will return to heal, in the integration, the wound created in the repression. The very nature of our being searches for healing, for wholeness.

We know this about individual psychology. We are beginning to recognize that the same truth holds in collective psychology - the vast reservoir of language, world views, myths, and motifs that provide interpretive meaning to our individual lives. Collectively, in the consciousness of humanity as a whole, that which is repressed will return to be heard, to be integrated in a wider synthesis and deeper healing.

According to most historical estimates, about five thousand years ago, for causes as yet unclear and probably not as malevolent as their consequences, the collective consciousness of humanity repressed all traces of the feminine aspects of spirit. That which had previously been honored, revered, and respected with awe was, within a fairly short period of time, not only devalued but denied. The Great Goddess, in her divine and human aspects, creator of life, source of the mystery, sacred sustainer and nurturer, doorway to wisdom and transformation, was pushed out of hearing, out of sight. Along with her, like a long trail on a comet, went respect for women and acknowledgment of the worth of feminine values and experience.

Those five thousand years encompassed colossal evolutionary strides for humanity. During that time, we moved from small, wandering horticultural groups, grasping tightly and superstitiously to a precarious survival, to a species that can photograph its own plant from a distant moon.

These five thousand years are the years of patriarchy. With the rise of patriarchy, world views became saturated with only masculine images of the sacred as well as with predominantly masculine values: power, dominance, control, and separation. There is some sense of evolutionary necessity in the reign of such values since power, dominance, and control help assure survival in a holistic environment and separation is a necessary, although temporary, step in the movement to deeper understanding. It could be argued that, although they quickly began to grow cancerous, these particular traits and values allowed and enabled the emergence of reason and its offspring - the sciences, arts, philosophies, and technologies. Indeed, this era saw the emergence of the world's great religions, our wisdom traditions. Growth in human consciousness during those five hundred centuries of patriarchy defined civilization as we still know it and human awareness, communication, and relationships to each other as well as to the universe as we still live it.

In its devaluation of half of humanity and half of the qualities of the sacred, the patriarchal world view we've inherited has put a limit on what a human being can know and what a human being can be. All of the achievements, accomplishments, and insights into the nature of our phenomenal world, into the nature of our sacred ultimate reality, nature of human beings and our place in that phenomenal world and ultimate reality are founded in a world view that had excluded half of the dimensions of the lived human experience. The patriarchal world view went so far out of balance that, in eliminating half of the dimensions of the sacred, it eliminated the sacred itself. The era, ushered in with the dictum, "The Goddess is dead," ended at its outermost limits with the equally meaningless, "God is dead." What was dead was that particular world view's usefulness in encompassing reality.

As in any act of repression, individual or collective, what is repressed will be heard and demand integration. We are always moving toward wholeness, always longing for it. Any world view that disallows wholeness will find its own end. Such is the time in which we live. Power, dominance, control, and separation have come to the limit of their exclusive utility. They have created problems that cannot be solved within a world view that knows no other solutions.

Our time cries out for the qualities of all that has been repressed and the inclusion of those qualities in a vaster, more integrated awareness of being. At the end of the dominance of agency, we need to integrate the communion of relatedness. At the end of the exclusivity of reason, we need to integrate the balance of intuition and other forms of non-conceptual knowing. At the end of hierarchical control, we need to integrate mutually nurturing co-existence. And, at the end of being lost in the outer world, we need to integrate awareness of the radiance, peace, and confidence offered inwardly.

Fortunately, patriarchy's dismissal of the feminine aspects of the sacred did nothing to affect the living reality of the feminine aspects of the sacred. They have always been here. Over the centuries, a few have heard the voice of Mary or Vajrayogini or glimpsed Kali or Kwan Yin. For the most part, however, a patriarchal world view allowed its members only a limited spectrum of sight and sound. It does seem as if the feminine aspects of the sacred are calling more loudly to us now, like a lighthouse sending urgent signals to a lost ship. Or, perhaps, having reached the limits of patriarchal thinking and witnessing the breakup of the reign of its world view, we simply have more holes in the veil through which we have seen the world. We can now get a better view of the sacred feminine that has been here all along.

One day a few years ago, I was pulling into a parking spot, just going through the errands of my life. I had been thinking for a long time about the emergence of the divine feminine in the collective consciousness. I found myself, in that instant of stopping the car, also stopped - in my own awareness - by an intense experience of presence. In a profound moment that was both humbling and empowering. I heard an inner voice say, "Yes. Right. In you. You are part of the collective consciousness. I am emerging in you."

We are beginning to hear it all around us. The divine feminine, repressed for so long, is speaking out now. She speaks both of her desire and capacity for healing - loudly and lyrically and boldly and lovingly and sensuously and powerfully and in a multitude of voices. One of those voices is Sam Oliver's.

Introduction

As mysterious as the dark side of the moon, lies a hidden force of nature embedded within us all. It is the nurturing side of our being containing seeds of awareness awaiting to be born. It lies within the silent spaces between our thoughts. It is a pregnant silence with infinite possibilities.

Within these seeds of awareness is the womb of creation. It feels like a loving mother whose soul purpose is to unconditionally love what comes into being. Out of this spacious quality of life are invisible bonds. These invisible bonds create a sense of security. A sense of knowing we are loved by a power greater than ourselves. This power guides us and sustains us. And, it is filled with enough love to carry us through each day.

Rooted within this love is a quality of attention. This quality of attention is reflective. It is a glimpse of our Creator. As we observe this pathway into love. Our soul is bathed in the very wisdom that created it.

This book is about integrating the feminine spirit. At the same time, it is the process of returning to our birthright. Each of us wants to know we are loved. We long for such grace.

All of us know that the world cannot promise us this notion of being loved.

Only our soul can carry us into a dimension in life whereby the unseen becomes more real than the appearances of our lives. In this regard, we move into the eternal nature of living that fears nothing and has the experience of a thousand lifetimes. Like a child, we are to live each moment as though it was new. When we are open to life's mysteries, we follow the feminine spirit. It is the pathless path of spirit calling us home.

Everyone can remember a time in their life when a mother or a father called them in to eat dinner. Far more than a dinner is being prepared. Together, the children and the loving parent(s) gather at a table to eat a meal. This meal is a communal act. In the act of eating a meal, every person participating is filled with the bounty of mother earth. In essence, it is she that provided the meal we all partake of daily. Within every bite digested is a remembering that we are children of earth.

The bounty of the earth is nurtured by a living presence we cannot see. This unseen presence infuses our lives with the experience of opportunity. Every moment is an opportunity to remember who we are. As we remember who we are, we are integrating our lives, and yes, our souls into the seasons and cycles of living. At the same time, we have a part of us not affected by birth and by death.

Thus, the cycles of birth and death become a symbol. A symbol to remind us how sacred we are. In this realization, we are integrated into a multitude of possibilities available to us at any given moment. This infinite array of choices carries diverse connections from one moment to another until our choices extend into endless streams of possibilities. This circle that goes on and on connects our humanity to the womb of creation whereby we are always cared for by the love of the feminine spirit.

As we move into the 21st century, it will become vital that the feminine spirit flourish. The feminine side of humanity nourishes and encourages active participation of our soul in the world. And, I'm not sure we can keep from moving in this direction. Daily, we can watch the news. People are killing each other for material wealth and power. We fight for higher prices on goods and services. These higher prices are justified by stating we are meeting our external desire to succeed in the world. Often, our desire to flourish in the external world is at the expense of insight and inner reflections on love.

In our day, our souls are crying out to be blessed, known, loved, and wanted. The external world cannot guarantee this. The internal world of insight can. Insight means to see from within. As we turn our awareness within, we return to our feminine nature. Our feminine nature turns our attention toward the qualities of purity, hope, and spirit. They are the qualities of our nature that intend goodness and love.

It is my hope and prayer that our society learns to value being in the process of living, more so, than living for the results. Otherwise, we cannot appreciate living the lives we have been given in the present moment. When "being in process" is given as much attention as "results," there is an opportunity for our actions to mirror our own soul seeking the manifestation of peace within our world. In so doing, the feminine spirit is born.

Here, our daily experiences begin to sustain us at the deepest level of our being. We become grateful for each moment as an opportunity to care for what gives us meaning and joy. In return, our soul is healed by the very spirit that brings all life into being. When we feel connected to this quality of ourselves, we take on the spirit of a child. In our childlike nature, we trust the forces of nature that has shaped the moon, the sky, and our well-being. It is not a part of us we can easily see, but this part of us becomes more vital to us as we age.

As we mature, we begin to realize that our five senses and physical body will fade. What remains will be what cannot be seen. It is the part of us born into the world, leading us to this moment, and leading us into eternity. The feminine side of our lives is soulful. We are free within our soul. Even death cannot diminish the birth of our soul.

In the end, we begin to trust our heart as well as our visual perceptions. Then, our soul is at home in the world. When we view our world with the eyes of soul, our external world is bathed in eternal love. What is united becomes an integration of the feminine spirit into the external world from within.

Have you ever thought of the earth as energy, or the air we breathe as being similar to ambiotic fluid breathed during pregnancy? One early morning, I was sitting on my front porch looking at the grass. I saw waves of energy rising from the ground and into the air.

In a similar way, we each enter into the womb of another creation the moment we leave our human mother's womb. It could be said that we never really leave our real mother's womb-the feminine spirit. Each event, circumstance, and experience is an opportunity to integrate a loving presence in our lives. We breathe her in.

This loving presence nurtures us constantly. We are bathed in her womb constantly. She is a spacial quality within us that is blessed, known, and caring for. This quality of attention is not bound by any physical form. It is the part of us that is limitless. It is the part of us experiencing our world in purity. It is our soul.

Our soul is fluid and without form. It has the capacity to pierce through the veils of flesh and bones. Our soul is soft. This tender part of our existence is not caught up in being the strongest, richest, or even the most self-righteous. Our soul simply rests in what is. It does not get caught up in one's or another's personality. Our soul sees people and ourselves as children of the cosmos with unique attributes creating our very existence on earth.

Viewing our lives through soul reveals a quality of attention within us not determined by external circumstances. Our soul is the aspect of us hidden behind the conditions or circumstances we find ourselves in. Our soul is the eternal and unconditional quality of our being that will never die.

The Story behind the Book

Have you ever had an idea that would not let you go? Something inside you that just had to come out? This book is one of these experiences. Late one night, I was sleeping. In the middle of the night, I was awakened. Inside my thoughts were the words "Integrating the Feminine Spirit...Integrating the Feminine Spirit...Integrating the Feminine Spirit." These four words simply went through my mind over and over. Finally, after about an hour that seemed like days, I rose out of my bed to write these four words down on a piece of paper. Then, I was able to fall into a deep sleep.

The next morning, I woke up and read these four words that would not let me sleep the night before. Little did I know that this morning I would write the introduction to "Integrating the Feminine Spirit." In many ways, this book is a continuation of my first one titled, "What the Dying Teach Us: Lessons on Living." Although the theme of this book is unique, I have reflected deeply on my work with dying Hospice patients. As a Spiritual Counselor for The Center for Hospice and Palliative Care, Inc. in South Bend, IN, I witness dying patients enter into a womb like state.

As a dying patient closes his or her eyes to the world around them, they enter deeply into themselves. Within each of us is a vast array of experiences moving us deeper and deeper into the realization just how sacred our lives are. I wrote the following poem to my female friends at Hospice. It contains elements of expressions you will hear me speak of in the contents of this book. The title of this poem is: **The Heart of a Woman.**

The heart of a woman
flows
as a waterfall
descending
like a torrent
down a steep mountain.

Plunging into an abyss
deeper and deeper
creating waves
expanding its inner tides
vibrating into being
the movements of a dance.

Flowing freely
through endless streams
each vibration
extends
into the heart
of all.

This vast array of purity

anoints

those entering its path

bathing

in the Spirit of a woman

whose heart reveals her soul.

Sam Oliver

In each of our lives, there are times when we want to close our eyes and enter into this womb like state. It is the desire to enter into the feminine spirit where we are blessed, seen as good, wanted, and loved. The feminine side of our being creates a sense of being cared for that the world around us cannot. When we enter into her presence, we are entering into wisdom and creation.

Any work of art, manuscript, play, or movie is created out the feminine spirit's intent to bring into manifestation the deepest longings of a person's soul. She does not do this with conditions. The conditional world is the world around us we seek to find our identity in. Yet, to really know who we really are requires the intent to seek out what cannot be seen. As we enter into the world of insight, the ability to see from within, we are entering into this wisdom that created us.

The Feminine aspect of our Creator moves us into the world of contemplation. Our ability to be aware of our awareness is a tremendous gift. When we witness and feel the privilege of being fully human, we are given the opportunity to experience our spirit in flesh and blood. We are given the opportunity to experience the created order of our Creator continuing to draw us into our natural state. Dying patients come very close to this natural state of who we really are. Babies entering into the world through the womb of creation offer a level of insight into bliss and the experience of connectedness to a greater birth taking place beyond the physical aspects of birth. For within every birth lies a mother and a father whose participation with the feminine spirit forever alters their identity.

In a real way, a newly mother and father are transformed. He or she will never think the same again. And, living to meet one's own needs no longer becomes possible on the deepest levels of our being. I have been fortunate to encounter the feminine spirit two times with my son Luke and my daughter Emilee's birth. They are precious beings to me and inspire me to become a better person every day. Presently, Luke and Emilee are in their preteens. They have an innocense about them that helps me remember my place in the world as a child - a child of The Creator whom I call God.

My children touch me in places of my heart that help me identify with my natural state to trust an inner knowing inside me. It is my identification with life that transcends all the appearances of this world. This life inside me is eternal and far more real than anything I will ever encounter in this world. All that comes into being moves through this spacial conscious awareness inside us. The feminine spirit brings forth life from nothingness. She has the capacity to give hope to the blind, set free the captives of his/her mind and emotions, inspire great things from ordinary people like you and me, and give us the courage to see through the veil of death into life eternal. Sooner or later, each of us will take this path. It is a journey that will lead us into the heart of God.

Part One: The Growth of Insight

The Innocence of a Child

Each day I witness my son Luke and my daughter Emilee grow. They are constantly learning something new. Every moment, they are open to every possibility available to them. They have no reason to judge or interpret anything. Life and experience are simply manifestations of magical experiences that open their hearts and minds to be captivated by the wonders of creation.

I can see this happening in my own life. The first time I saw Niagra Falls I was speechless. My entire attention was focused in that moment. I was totally in the experience, rather than, analyzing it. In a sense, I became the waterfall. I could identify with it. I could feel it move through me. I could feel the calmness in the midst of rushing water. I could feel the coolness of the water in my body. My mind simply observed. And, for a brief moment, Sam no longer existed. I was just as much the waterfall as I was Sam. In fact, a close identity with ourselves alone keeps us from the innocence of a child.

A newborn child has to learn its name. And, a child has to learn what will hurt them and what experiences to avoid. All of this is necessary, and yet, a child longs to be free. Our children do come through us, but they are not really ours. They belong to the Universe.

In a real way, you and I are children of the cosmos even if we have forgotten. We long to return to the childlike nature

2

within us that views every moment and every opportunity as a mysterious gift. And, the moment we greet each encounter with the innocence of a child, we return to our natural state.

To be in harmony with the creative flow of the Universe, we have to remember our innocence. In this realm, our exterior lives do not determine our destiny. Innocence reminds us that our life is determined by what we become open to within us. Here, the wonder of a child infuses each experience with the blessings of unconditional love. In so doing, the act becomes an anointing from our Creator. What is born in this anointing is a sense of meaning beyond the mind and the heart's capacity to comprehend.

This anointing creates a path. It is a channel of expression uniting the divine with the human. What is experienced will be determined by how much or how long we choose to remain on this path. We will encounter people, places, and events that are incarnations of the past inner choices made to draw into us the life, in which, we now find ourselves.

Inside each of us is the innocense of a child. We are not the interpretations of our body. We are not even the body. Nor, can we even be what we think we are. We are far more than we know. We are sons and daughters of a Creator who has given us infinite choices. What lies within each choice is unconditional love. This unconditional love is eternal and full of grace. This is our home. This is the innocence of a child.

"My imagination is my Doctor." These were the words of my five-year-old son Luke. Emilee had hurt her toe, and I told my daughter that Luke and I would send her foot love. "It would be like mailing a letter of love to her grandparents," I said. Moments later, I asked Emilee how her foot was doing. She said, "it was better."

Just after Emilee's comment on feeling better, Luke said, "Dad, my imagination is my Doctor." I was filled with joy at my son's insight. In a real way, Luke and I were using our imagination to be an invisible link between the healing power of love within us and our desire for Emilee to be free of pain. And, she received it well.

This reminds me of e-mail. We live in a time where we can instantly think of someone, type in our thoughts of them on a computer, send these thoughts through the airwaves, and become aware that these thoughts are being received many miles away. We can imagine how the person receiving our envelopes of love will read them externally and internally. The instant our imagination is connected to our thoughts and feelings we will have entered soul. Here, the appearance of separateness fades into eternal bonds embraced through insight.

What do you think would happen if we lived our lives in a similar way just described? What if we were to live our lives in a way that what cannot be seen is more real than what can be seen? And, could it be possible that hidden behind all appearances of reality is an inner vision of one's intentions and desires revealing themselves?

Hidden behind our experiences is an opportunity to envision the motivations and the language of our souls. What is revealed becomes a symbol. It is a tangible expression of a person's awareness of life. It is one's soul seeking to be born from what cannot be seen. What comes forth from this spacial quality within us is the heart of a child. A child of the cosmos seeking to be loved and wanted.

To the child of innocence, everything is magical. It is often called the "beginner's mind." Adults experience this each time we move to a new home, a new job, or a new relationship. We tend to look at our world and those in it with unconditional love.

Fear cannot enter a state of innocence. Our innocent state of being is the experience of being totally cared for and loved. Innocence is a childlike state, whereby, we live in total bliss. Our world from this quality of our being is whole.

Innocence is like a great day when all is in flow. The events, circumstances, and inner reflections on our lived experience are in unity. On these days, there is nothing anyone can say or do to keep us from our goals, desires, hopes, and dreams.

This state of being allows us to experience the spiritual aspect of ourselves. What we desire and intend moves in and through us like a river making its way through a channel into the open sea. There is no separation from what we think we are and who we really are. Our awareness and personality, infused by spirit, are united.

The Innocence of a Child

Inside every person
lies the heart of a child
filled with innocence
expressing itself in the world.

This inner connectedness
supercedes appearances
for to become it
move us into soul.

Nothing can touch
our child within
as we travel
the path of spirit.

Thus, what cannot be touched
touches all
with endless streams of consciousness
forever linked by un-conditioned love.

Sam Oliver

Personal Notes

Sam Oliver

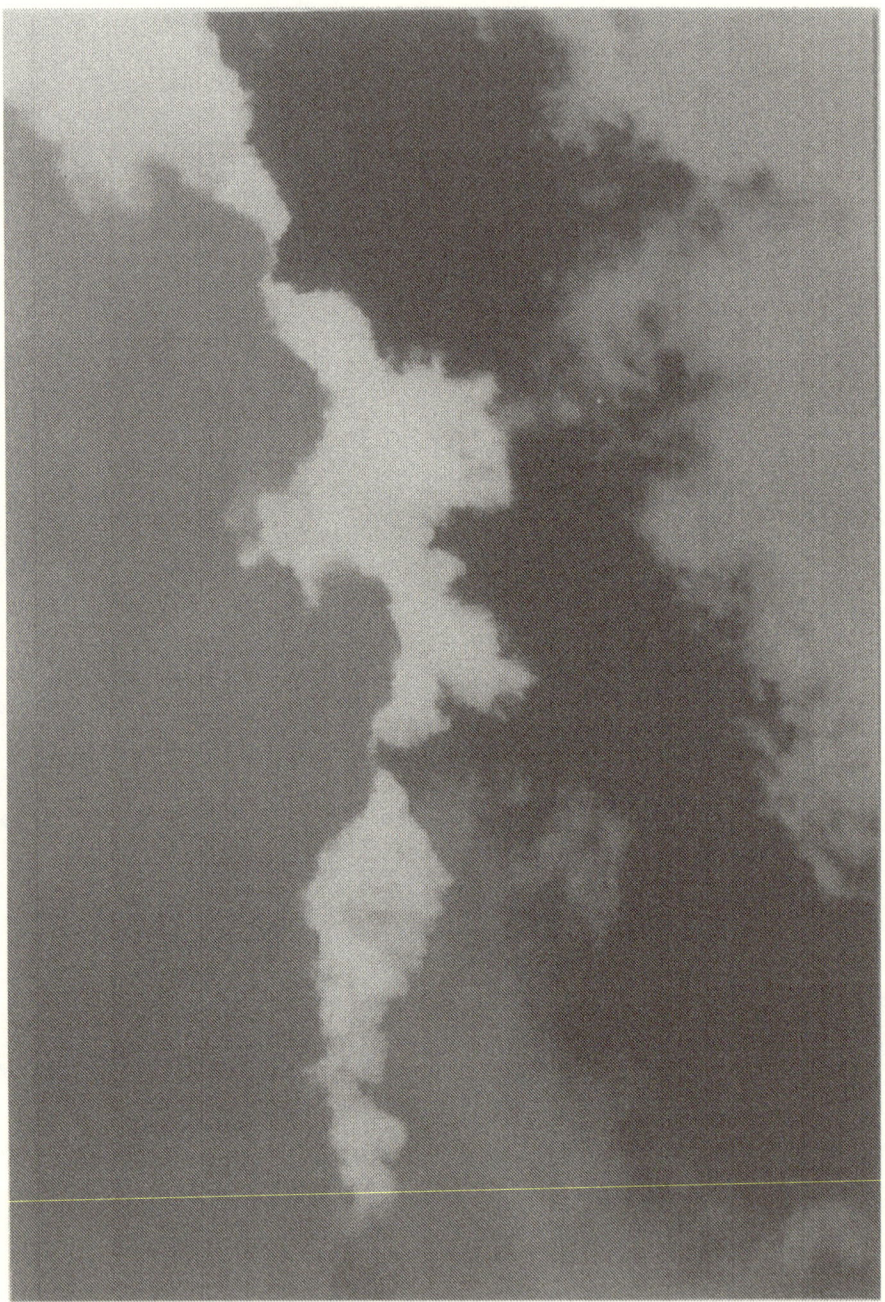

The Loss of Purity

As we mature, we begin to realize that the world we live in isn't what it appears to be. Within every encounter, word, and deed lies subtle encounters, words, and deeds. At this point, we begin to notice a dualistic tendency. Inside us, we struggle because our inner child hasn't had to face anything beyond total unity. Once our inner child is born, it has distanced itself from unity consciousness. Then, a loss of purity emerges, and the search for one's soul is ignited.

This dualism occurs when people begin to hide behind roles, interpretations, and judgements. And, when people begin to use their roles, interpretations, and judgements to define us, we begin to question who we are for the first time. What began as an assumption about our true nature is being challenged.

At this point, the birth of our external self calls our attention outside us. It is a movement from within to what lies outside us. As we take on a myriad of roles, interpretations, and judgements to be more authentic than our true nature (inner child), we feel this loss deep in our soul. This movement from our authentic self to our public self has the potential of creating a split between our inner and outer persona unless our public self becomes consistent with our inner self. If our external self is not consistent with who we are inside, there is a tremendous loss of personal identity.

Each of us has a personal identity or awareness we bring into this world. We view the world in a way no one else has, can, and ever will. Our authentic voice is vital. Our uniqueness adds life, variety, and wholeness to our world of so many viewpoints.

It is important that we integrate our authentic presence into everything we are and do. If this is not done, there is a sense of confusion. We take on roles, definitions, and experiences others want us to live through their understanding of us. Thus, allowing others to control our destiny. Our soul will lose its way in the world, and we cry out for release. We cry out for release from a world that continues to determine our destiny in ways that pull us further from innocence. The further we move away from our innocence due to living the interpretations of other people's perceptions, the more we lose sight of who we are. Our heart aches. We are broken.

A child is born into a world of form from the formless. Children are inherently in tune with their essential nature. They cannot say where they begin or where they end. To a child, they are at one with the universe. They feel at home.

Of course, our world is filled with the notion of separation, boundaries, and limits. It even looks that way. This dualistic idea instilled in the minds of children entering the material world hurts the self confidence of a child. The Higher Self confidence inside us knows we are all energy and information with skin stretched over us. Our body hides the field of intelligence that pervades all life.

At this point, a child begins to question their identity. She is encouraged to deny inner realities such as intuition and feelings in order to fit into society's tendency toward rational thought separating and defining our existence. Thus, the first layer of innocence is masked by a protective veneer. This mask begins to protect the innocence of a child. It is a layer of consciousness. In this layer of consciousness, fear is introduced. The fear of extinction as though this new identity called humanity is all one can be. The consciousness of fear is embraced in order to fit into the world.

As a child grows, he accumulates multiple layers of consciousness hiding his authentic self. Occasionally, a child will catch a glimpse of its true nature, and the experiences of joy and sorrow rise within us. This dichotomy creates an external and internal tension. And, the dance between these worlds of form and formless become more and more refined and understood.

When our life is split in this way, an identity is created outside us sometimes known as a persona. Now, our identity can be viewed outside us. Here, a personality is developed. This personality is the part of us we show to the public. It is the part we use to shield ourselves from fully expressing our soul. It is the part of us that covers what we desire the most. It is the part of us that keeps us from returning to spirit.

11

It was a hot and sunny day, and I was riding in my car with Luke and Emilee. About 100 yards ahead of us was steam rising from the road. Emilee saw what I saw and said, "Look, there is water on the road."

My intellect and experience wanted to correct my daughter, who was then six years old, whose thoughts of water on the road came from a place in her awareness just as correct as mine. Yes, she will learn some day about steam rising from the road, but her consciousness is in a different place right now. I believe Emilee was expressing more in her imagination along with the experience of a six-year-old intellect. She was comprehending this experience from her own level of understanding. It was pure and innocent. She was not told her experience of this water was wrong or even flawed.

I had a choice to make at this point. I could correct Emilee and draw her to my level of understanding. Or, I could meet Emilee where she was and trust divinity to guide her to more understanding of this as she ages.

In a real way, we all live in our own little world and believe the world revolves around our concepts and notions of what we think it is. In our own world, we experience purity. We feel that our own way of living in the world is good, that is, until someone else imposes another train of thought into our thoughts.

Here, we are faced with a dilemma. We are forced to accept another person's view of the world we perceive to be a certain way, or hold on to our own. Sometimes we trust our own view and discount the views of others. Either way, our own way of thinking has been integrated into the collective consciousness of our world views. And, we begin to question our own sense of self and purity.

The Loss of Purity

In a world of perceptions,

there are various views,

by which, we encompass our world

and live its qualities.

It is our nature as humans

in clinging to thoughts

as ultimate expressions of reality

yet to be shifted by life.

As we let go of what we think life is

acknowledging the limits of thought

and giving way to what's highest in us

the loss of purity begins to fade.

Sam Oliver

Personal Notes

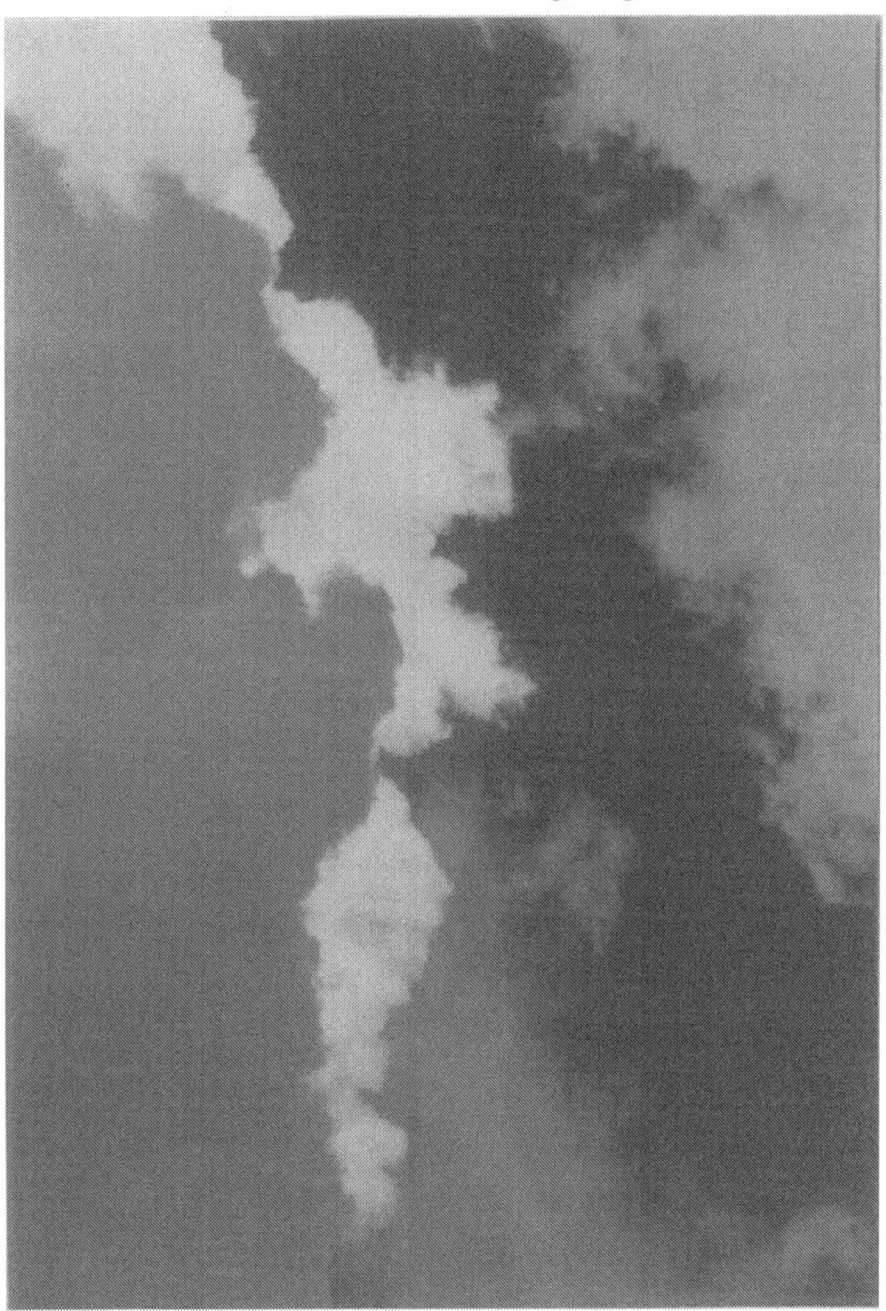

A Broken Heart

In my work at Hospice, I visit many patients and families whose hearts are broken through the pain of death. Death symbolizes many experiences. One is the death of a dream. Many patients and families have hopes and dreams to create certain life experiences with their mate and family. When these dreams are held at bay and are coming to a close in death, a broken heart begins to replace the dream and the hopes of mates and their families.

This is also the case in our own lives. When life does not go as we planned, there is a feeling of loss. It feels like every atom in our body is breaking apart. Our heart feels sad. Our mind is confused and lacking direction.

During this time, we can feel that our life is no longer purposeful. We begin to hide our heart from ever getting hurt again. This notion is useless, and we know it. Even if we pull away from the pain of others, we cannot hide from the pain of knowing life is a series of gains and losses.

Our losses can become dominant in our life if we cut off this opportunity to feel, reflect, and become acquainted with our grief. In grief, our heart hurts. It feels like it is being split into two parts. The first part represents our past. The second part represents our future.

The first part of a broken heart is characterized by losing a portion of our life that has brought us to this moment of sorrow.

16

We begin to remember the joys and sorrows of our life with the one(s) we loved. Each moment becomes more than a memory. Each experience becomes a living presence in our heart.

When the death of a physical relationship or experience becomes apparent, a rush of energy floods this first part of a broken heart. As the intensity of loss unfolds, this energy enables us to be sustained by a power greater than ourselves. Here, we are held in a nurturing bond we cannot see.

The second part of a broken heart represents our future. At this point, we begin to envision a life without the one(s) we loved. Sometimes, we begin to feel guilty about this part of our heart. We do not feel we have a right to feel anything but sorrow during a time of loss. This is why a heart can feel as though it is breaking, and filled with hope at the same time. Somehow, this gives us a balancing of energies within to sustain us.

Between the joys and sorrows of a broken heart is an empty space. It is the sacred space of seeking. This spacial quality within us uncovers the landscape of our soul moving to envelop our heart with strength beyond its perceived sense of self. We are filled with spirit and infused with power to find peace in the midst of despair.

This spacial quality where our soul (awareness) is infused by spirit (eternal love) is freeing to a person experiencing a sense of loss giving us hope for the future. Our heart is held in this quality of our being. We reflect on this movement realizing

17

this part of our experience will never die. Our pain becomes a strengthening of our soul. Our soul is empowered by the source of its life. And, divinity brings our attention into the light of hope. At this point, we begin to listen with our heart. Our heart knows the way to this peace beyond understanding.

In a world where families are breaking apart due to deaths, divorces, children killed in gangs, etc., our hearts are being ripped into. It becomes increasingly difficult to consider our family as a place where we can be in refuge from the rest of our world. It is as though there are no more boundaries in a place the world once could not penetrate. Thus, our hearts are broken by this unseen force entering the consciousness of every home.

We are left to pick up the pieces the best way we can. In the face of hopelessness, we long to find hope. The result is a myriad of hearts broken by the chaos around us, and now, in us. It is as though we are all receiving a lesson on evolution. Evolution teaches us that what comes into being, must someday, come to an end. In the end, we become One with what brings all life into being.

This sadness filling our heart is great, and we begin to look within for strength. As our awareness moves to the center of our broken heart, we search for guidance. We move through multi-layers of existence within us: we move through the pain of losses that have encompassed our lives to this moment, we move through the losses we had hoped for, and we grieve the loss of using up this present moment with what demands our attention. At the end of this journey, a broken heart enters into emptiness.

Imagine living your life so close to a person that you share the same heart beat, the same thoughts, the same feelings, and the same bodily fluids. Such is the case of a baby in the womb of its mother. Each breath is a channel of life drawn in to connect with a small child waiting to be born. All this child could ever need and want is dependent on its mother's care.

Then, it comes. It is time for this child to be born. The sum of this child's human experience, thus far, has been sustained by the love of its mother. Now, this child has to let go of all it has known in order to be born. For the first time, a child has to contemplate a life outside its mother's womb. The beginning of a personal identity develops. The known becomes a mystery. The unknown is embraced.

The child has been a part of a world it has loved. As this child enters a brave new world, this child carries with him a sense of being loved beyond human understanding. On the one hand, she grieves the loss of a comfortable world no longer available to her. On the other hand, her adventuresome spirit of a child's soul knows it has to move on to embrace its destiny. As her heart is broken, an outpouring of peace deep within her creates a path. It a path not able to be seen, but it is vividly felt as real inside us. It is the path of spirit.

Along this spiritual path, a child enters a world filled with adventure and mystery. There is a peace within this path creating invisible links into the unseen world. It has a similar feeling to that of a loving mother holding the hand of a frightened child. It is the peace filled love of the feminine spirit carrying a child through the fear of the unknown and into the freedom of its most authentic self.

A Broken Heart

A divided heart
separated by two different worlds
contain various perceptions
held close to our heart.

This dualistic tendency
to live a fractured existence
tears our heart
into a myriad of pieces.

The brokenness
shattered by what was
calls forth our soul
from the depths of infinity.

From sacred humanness,

our heart emerges

rising to become

its most authentic power.

Sam Oliver

Personal Notes

Part Two: The Infusion of Spirit

The Experience of Emptiness

Emptiness is transitory. It is a spacial quality within us that is neither running away from nor moving toward an experience. It occurs when we are leaving one life experience and moving into another.

This journey has a unique purpose. It has a way of helping us remember how infinite we are behind our physical bodies and minds. As spiritual beings having a human experience, this journey into emptiness connects us to our essence. When we retrieve our authentic presence, we draw to us a sense of sacredness.

As human beings, we fear this journey into emptiness. We fear losing sight of concrete descriptions of ourselves. We fear losing our external identities such as: mother, father, sons, daughters, friends, boss, etc ... Yet, these roles are simply incarnations from our essence (spirit), rather than, our essence. These external aspects of our being have qualities of attention that are temporal. If our existence is dependent on our external states of being, we will fear losing any of these qualities of attention. We will lose everything we know.

Underneath our roles and experiences are mystical sides of us. It is the part of us that knows no fear. It is free of definitions and labels used to define us. And, it has the capacity to carry our consciousness from what we know to the unknown.

This path into the unknown has a cleansing effect. All our joys and sorrows are washed away into a sea of bliss. Our inner life is not pulled into life's circumstances in sorrow or in joy. It is here we center our awareness into the "I" becoming a "We." It is a journey from our personal awareness of our self into a universal consciousness of the "I" centered in a collective conscious awareness that is "We."

When we enter into the collective conscious awareness of all that has, is, and ever will be, we are moved to look even deeper. Behind the "We" is the source of all life. When we are centered in what brings life into being, we are fully integrated in the universe. Uni-verse or "one song" is a single vibration that extends itself into endless streams of consciousness. This vibration is harmonious and moving. Our soul is touched, and we are bathed in the experience of emptiness being filled with the awareness of our true self. In the end, we discover our Creator as the manifestation of emptiness taking on physical form and returning to itself renewed and forever loved.

Emptiness has a purpose. It helps us to remember, or shall I say re-member ourselves back into the one verse, one song, or universe that is our home. Our spirit extends through our individual selves and into our external nature of what cannot be contained in any physical body. As we discover our Creator through the creative force underlying all appearances, we become what we've been all along - "children of the cosmos."

What if...I were to tell you I lived by a prostitute. Would you have immediate judgements about her? What if...I were to tell you I see many men come and go from her home all night. Would you begin to be angry or sorry for her? What if...I were to tell you this prostitute now has AIDS. Would you feel she deserved it? What if...I were to tell you the real prostitute was me. How would you feel about me?

Anyone who has judgements, anger, sorrow, or self-righteousness toward anyone living a life different from themselves has entered into the life of another through their perceptions we all are a part of. Our feelings, thoughts, and awareness become attached to another's view of the world, and we will have used their outer appearance to justify our own need to condemn another. In this sense, we are using the image, body, life of another to gain power over or separate ourselves from a fellow soul. In an attempt to separate ourselves from what cannot be, our unity behind all diversity is lost. In these realms of reality, the prostitute and those who label her as such are one.

In letting go of judgements, labels, concepts, feelings, thoughts, etc., we enter into an eternal expression of relationships not defined by our external masks covering our authentic self. In simple awareness, there are no labels and judgements. In simple awareness, we care for each other's soul. In simple awareness, we are one.

Emptiness means to let go of our preconceived notions of ourselves and others. When we let go of what we think is true, we enter into the dimension of inspiration and revelation. We enter the domain of our awareness where the thoughts and feelings we have toward others and life come from mystery and intrigue; rather than, places in our heart filled with concepts defining what will always be less than our deepest selves.

Early 1999, I went through a divorce. I never thought I would ever face such a thing in my entire life, but I did. My whole world was removed from me. Everything I had experienced in this marriage was part of my identity. It was all drifting away like a stick floating down a creek. The further my identity as a husband slipped away, the emptier I felt inside.

What was once filled with memories, hopes, and dreams with a marriage partner became an empty void. I felt like I had lost direction in life. A huge empty space began to occupy a space inside my heart once filled with experiences as a united family unit.

What would my future hold? Who would I meet? Would I want to meet anyone else? These questions began to occupy my empty space within my heart, mind, and soul. The asking of these questions deepened something inside me. There were no answers to these questions that would satisfy my longing to know. These questions served as a way of entering more fully into the depths life has to offer.

The deeper my awareness became inside me, the deeper I felt cared for by a power greater than myself. At one point, my thoughts and feelings of my loss began to fade. Their intensity diminished, and I began to feel a single and continuos vibration. I felt completely loved.

Then, a more subtle awareness came into my consciousness. I began to rest my attention in an infinite silence behind my feelings of awareness. I entered into a path paralleling my present circumstances. It was my emergence into spirit. I had returned home.

The Experience of Emptiness

Between what was,

and that yet to be

lies an empty space

waiting to be filled.

This spacial quality

opens our awareness

for spirit to appear

revealing a path.

As the path opens,

we are drawn near

to explore it

one step at a time.

Sam Oliver

Personal Notes

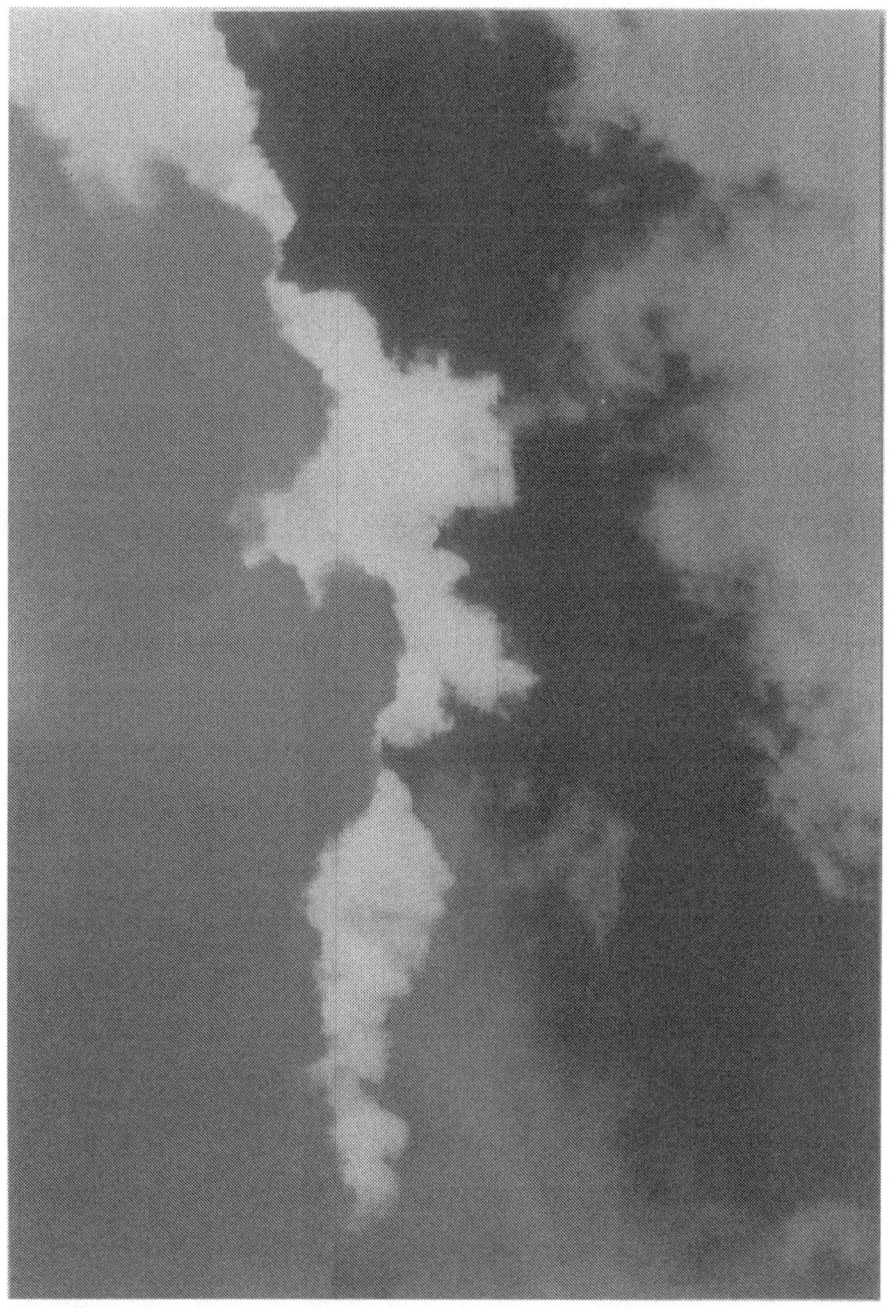

Dying into Life

Many people consider the ceasing of our thoughts and the end of a beating heart to be the end. Yet, this is really just the beginning of eternal life. Our lives are filled with endings and beginnings. They are continuos cycles moving in and through us endlessly.

As our perceptions and feelings about our self fades, we are left with an awareness of our own awareness. Eventually, our individual awareness becomes aware of our connection to the universe. When our individual awareness blends into cosmic awareness, we leave behind individual perceptions and feelings about what we are and merge into what cannot be contained in our perceptions and feelings. In this moment, we become more soul than body/mind. We are totally free. We have died into life. The interesting part of this notion is that we do not have to literally die in order to experience eternal life. It is the same intelligence bringing life into this moment, carrying us through this moment, and leading us home.

In a real way, there is nothing any of us really "do." We are all here to "be." Any time we believe we are doing anything, we are caught in the appearances of living. We are in dualism. We will have taken the illusions of our lives to be more real than what flows through us. And, the actions and experiences emerging from this level of awareness leaves our ego behind to do the work our Creator wants us to participate in. Thus, we die to our individual selves and become fully immersed in our purpose.

As we turn our attention to our inner being, we turn our attention toward loving guidance, experiences, and expressions of reality that will not die. Close your eyes for a moment. As the pictures in our outer world fade, there are inner visions within us that begin to form out of the formless. There is life inside us. When we close our eyes to what we know and look within for life to be revealed, we awaken into soul. As our inner life (awareness/soul) and outer lives (personality) merge, a level of congruency begins to take shape. Then, we are taking steps toward following a soulful path in manifested form.

When we cross over to immortality, we realize the journey from here to there is a shift in our attention. Here, our soul is in a dance with the appearances of our lives. We will have been infused by spirit to live through the longing of a person's soul uncovering another facet of itself.

Each dimension of our consciousness reveals another layer of awareness. The deeper we go into consciousness, the more we connect with multiple dimensions subtly residing within us. Eventually, we rest our awareness in a solitude of silence until we are totally immersed in being. Our own sense of being or personal awareness is gently integrated into universal consciousness. And, we are whole.

In this wholeness, we rest our lives. This is eternity. It is our natural state. In essence, it is the destiny of us all to let go of our physical awareness and definitions of what we think we are. At the end of letting go, we become fully integrated into what brings us life.

I meet many dying patients through my work at Hospice. They are generally very reflective by the time we meet. Hospice patients gather their memories, hopes, and dreams from their past, present, and future to lift them up to their Creator for mercy and blessing. They are looking over their life from birth to their dying. They recall past stories filled with thoughts, feelings, and images of their external expressions of living.

Each story reflects an inner longing to give meaning, value, and expression to what constitutes an individual collective awareness. As one tells his/her story, he begins to include the lives of others within him. These connections are invisible links forever forged within multiple lives interwoven in a single awareness.

As a person's physical expressions of living diminish, a person takes on a new identity born of spirit. It is a descent into the depths of one's inner being awakening insight. Insight, again, means to see from within. These inner visions are a collective link to our immortality. When we come to the end of our lives or any life experience, we begin to look within for direction and hope. It is an inner vision apart from what can be seen with our physical eyes.

When we look at our lives with a sense of inner vision, the appearances of our lives fall away. This falling away of external vision allows us to see our world through the eyes of compassion, mercy, and eternal love. As we do this, we become fully awake within ourselves. We will be soulful inside and out. We will embody spirit dying to what we "thought" we were at one time. Then, we are ready to become "bigger than life." We become infinite in our capacity to respond to the world with a co-creative purpose to fulfill.

It is our destiny to realize our full potential. It is the recognition we are more than our thoughts and feelings. In so doing, we are able to die into life. We move from self-centered awareness (body/mind) to life-centered awareness (body/mind/spirit) becoming fully integrated into the bonds of love that never end.

Out of a seedling, a flower grows. As it matures, its rose petals open revealing a hidden beauty. In its mature state, this openness is shared many ways. All who look upon its intricate portions find endless discoveries within it and themselves. These endless streams of connections illuminate an awareness within us. We become conscious of this flower's consciousness joining ours. And soon, we and the flower become one continuos flow of energy. We leave our awareness of a personal self in order to unite with a collective conscious awareness pervading all life.

This movement from self-centered awareness to life-centered awareness opens us to spirit. In spirit, life is revealed to us. It comes from within and beyond us. We get in touch with what brings all appearances of separateness into unity.

As we identify more with our essence, our identity with our personality begins to become less important to us. In the act of dying to our personality, we merge with what cannot die. This moment by moment movement into our destiny is like opening the petals of a flower. The deeper we go the more beauty we see inside us. Each layer uncovers more mysteries and more opportunities to discover levels of consciousness yet to be explored.

Dying into Life
The journey into life
is a series of losses
containing dying perceptions
of what we think we are.

It is a movement within us
creating inner pathways
connecting our soul
with eternity.

We are mysteriously guided
along these endless channels
expressing themselves uniquely
as infinite possibilities.

Behind each expression
lies at its center
a facet of our being
waiting to be born.

Sam Oliver

Personal Notes

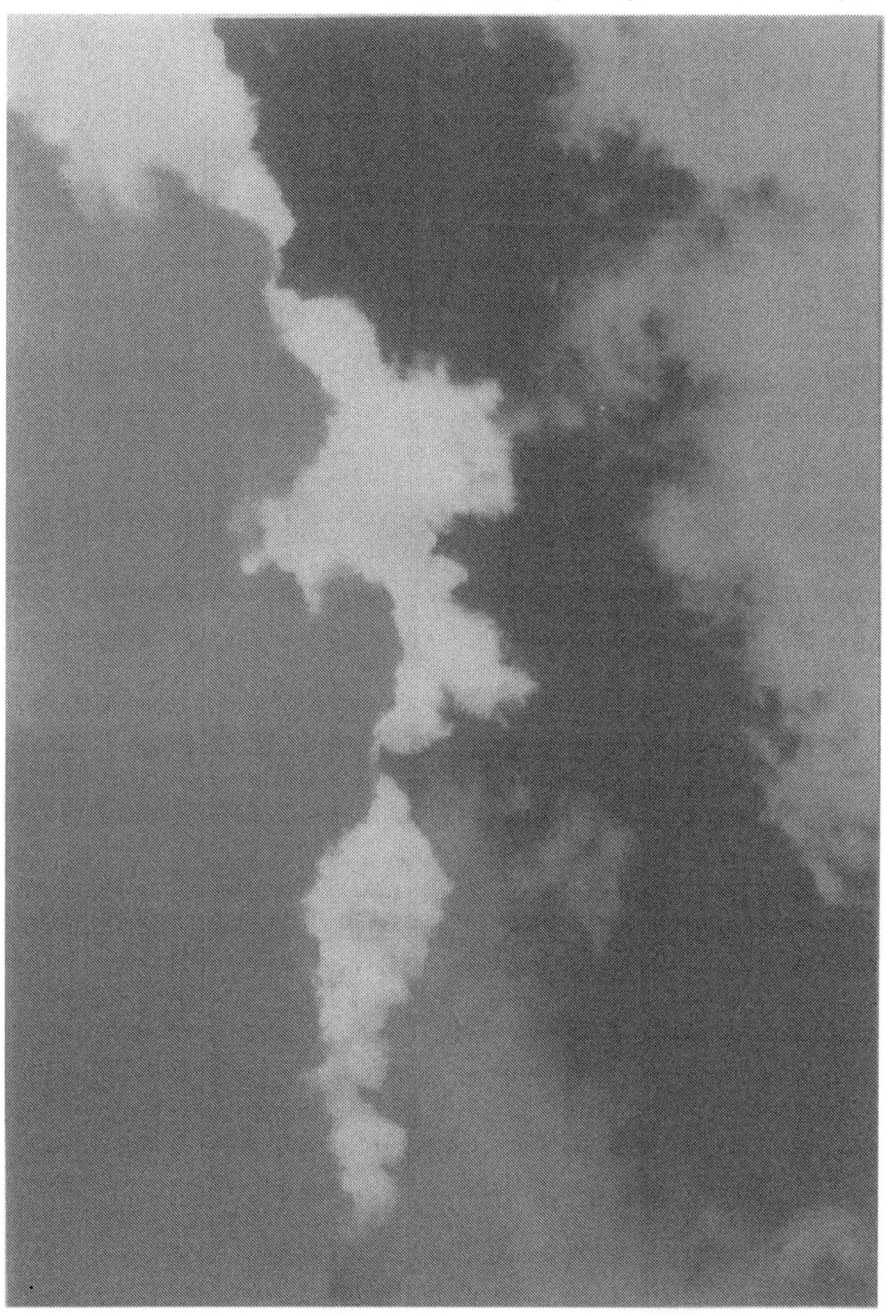

A Heart of Mercy

There comes a time in each of our lives when we begin to look deep within ourselves. Inside us is an infinite reservoir of faith, hope, and love. When the lives we live do not correspond to what we feel inside, we begin to draw out from within this reservoir. The result is an inner manifestation of our most authentic selves seeking congruency outside ourselves with what lies within.

A heart of mercy knows the appearances of our world are fragmented. A heart of mercy envisions what is possible for our world and works to infuse it with love. A heart of mercy is moved to act from unconditional love. A heart of mercy lives out of soul. A heart of mercy integrates soul into daily life.

In my work with dying patients, I am aware how other people's pain moves my heart. I begin to feel their brokenness with them. And, like a magnet, my heart goes out to them. Internal bonds are created. We are connecting. In this stream of consciousness, an awareness is incarnated. They become a part of me, and I am a part of them. For a brief moment in time, we are one. We are sharing in a relationship from the depths of our soul. Here, eternal relationships are formed.

Physical endings open us to life within. As our tears surface, we begin to grieve the loss of living through certain channels of expression. Our tears bring our exterior awareness into our heart. These tears become anointings of our heart integrating the life we've lived until it touches our soul. As these gentle closings deepen, we long to rest them in a spacial quality within us that is eternal and filled with mercy.

As the ending of a physical expression merges with one's tears reflecting the depths of life their soul has traveled, the relationships encountered in this awareness unite the sacred with the human. Our heart sinks into soul. We remember who we are. We remember the sacredness of our human relationships. We remember our essence. Most of all, we remember we are love made manifest by a power greater than ourselves.

There are constant influences in our world demanding our attention. Each has its own desires and intentions to express itself. All are contained in the world we choose to focus our attention on in any given moment. These desires have the capacity to divide our heart in many directions.

Within the center of every human heart lies a desire seeking to be known. It is a heart felt expression only the person holding it can let flow through. When we open ourselves to this aspect of ourselves, we open ourselves to our purpose for living. At this point, our soul is called out to express an aspect of our Creator. What flows from this desire to be known is a soulful expression. Our unique awareness is being called forth to become a connecting link between divinity and humanity.

Beyond all the joys and sorrows of daily living is a heart of mercy. A heart of mercy allows us to move forward through life

41

with a sense of purpose, grace, and unconditional love. A heart of mercy realizes that each moment is a gift and will never come to us in the same way again. Living in the present takes our full attention. As we become fully present, we become aware how grand our world really is. It is here we enter into mystery.

Our life is a mystery. None of us know for certain what the next minute will bring. Although each of us has an idea of what the future holds, our ideas are shaped and reshaped by the circumstances of our world. One thing is for certain. No one is ever alone. From one moment to the next, we are constantly guided by a heart of mercy deeply embedded in the feminine spirit.

A heart is a delicate part of a person's being. When we are joyful, our heart responds to this joy. When we are sad, our heart is moved to experience this as well. I'll never forget the first time I saw Luke and Emilee's heart beat on an ultrasound machine in the doctor's office. Although Luke and Emilee were not fully formed physically, their hearts were beating strong. Long before I saw their bodies, their hearts had become a part of mine. They were fully alive within me.

The same is true in any transformation. Trans-form means beyond form. In any change, there is great difficulty letting go of one's present experiences to take on a new one. Often, our heart goes ahead of us and the rest of us has to catch up. Our heart knows that life, in all its complexity, is a matter of trusting our heart to guide us.

Inside our heart, we are given indicators of how to proceed forward in any circumstance. Our heart contracts at experiences we perceive to be a threat to our physical well-being. Our heart is moved with great openness and passion toward experiences that will add zest to our lives. It is a trusted friend and guide on our path toward mercy.

A Heart of Mercy

In a world filled with pain,
we can sometimes feel
alone
and without hope.

It is an inner movement of our heart
rising above pain
igniting
an eternal fire.

This flame within us
intensely burns
creating
an open channel.

It is an invisible link

filled with mercy

connecting

our heart to Divinity.

This sacred-human relationship

protects our heart from

brokenness

that would shatter our soul.

Sam Oliver

Personal Notes

Part Three: The Return of Soul

An Awakened Heart

An awakened heart knows that the real journey of living is traveled within. Our exterior lives reflect a longing for our soul to be blessed, loved, and wanted. As our heart opens to new experiences, we begin to express ourselves differently. We become what we love. This creates an attachment with our heart. When our heart merges with a person, place, or thing, passion is created. This intense energy infuses our chosen experiences with a heart that has awakened to what lies before it.

An awakened heart knows there are endless paths. Each path contains different facets of one's own being. Underlying each awakening is a powerful force of nature. This underlying force nurtures us with an opportunity to express the longings of our heart to share what we have been given. Everyone has a unique gift. Our gifts are to be shared. Once shared, our gifts return to us emotionally like a reflection in a mirror. An awakened heart gives to others unselfishly knowing eternity is the ultimate gift giver.

An awakened heart feels the pain of its past, as well as, its joys. It is neither drawn into joy nor sorrow. Here, an awakened heart becomes steadfast. It can be trusted to lead us through life's ups and downs.

Once, we are able to stay centered in the midst of life's hills and valleys, the ebb and flow of our external world no longer

47

distract us from the pulse of our own heart feeling the vibrational sensations of its Creator.

As we awaken fully within ourselves, we are able to purposefully extend our heart, our passion, and our love into what we want to experience. This realization enables us to follow our heart because we know our soul will guide it into its desires. With the intention of good in all we do, our heart will awaken into a life experience filled with the awareness of co-creating with the Cosmos. In essence, an awakened heart will have returned home. It will have returned to love.

An awakened heart holds life at a balance between its mystery and our capacity to co-create our world. In co-creation, each of us has an idea about what we want out of life and a general knowledge of how to get there with the help of others. In mystery, we are constantly shifting our perceptions to deal with the obstacles that seem to be in the way of accomplishing our highest aspirations.

A heart that is awakened sees these obstacles as indicators. They indicate what demands our attention in life. On the level of soul, obstacles are not roadblocks. They are seeds of opportunity waiting for us to view them as information and energy capable of pulling us away from our highest intention.

An awakened heart sees these obstacles as illusions and lets them pass through. Once we are able to explore, experience, and feel these illusions without being drawn away from the fulfillment of our desire for wholeness, we are able to utilize mystery and co-creation to fulfill our ultimate desires. And, the path we are drawn into may not have been traveled the way we thought, but it will have become one guided by Spirit.

Here, an awakened heart rests in the joy of knowing it has found a home in the cosmos. It will awaken into the joy of being completely cradled in infinite love. This awakening has within it enough love to last a lifetime.

Life is a series of changes, losses, and gains. In its center, there is an emergence of an illuminating presence. It is an awakening of a constant flow of intelligence reminding us of our essential nature.

Behind our vibrations, our fluctuation of energy, and our senses is a settled sense of awareness not pushed and pulled by the various rhythms of life's experiences. It is a quality of our being marked by a sense of spaciousness and without form. This presence has the feeling of a heart opening itself to embrace joy.

Have you ever driven a car up a huge mountain or climbed one until you reached its peak? Then, stood at the top looking at the view. As you peeked over the mountain, you felt your chest begin to expand. As you breathed in the view, a part of you felt larger than your own life. At this time, you have become one with nature. You will have returned to nature, to which we are all connected to.

When we are open to take in all we can from the experience of a mountain, we look over the landscape from its entirety to its smallest detail. As we absorb the landscape and take it in, this experience now becomes a landscape within our own soul. Thus does an awakened heart feel the appearances of life's experiences within itself and recognizes itself in the other as one and the same.

An Awakened Heart

Throughout our lives
we engage in a series of events
leading to a crowning point
emerging through our heart.

Along this path,
a myriad of choices
transform us
from the depths of infinity.

An awakened heart
is aware of this ability
to connect with the rhythms of spirit
beating as one.

This desire to manifest

unity out of chaos

reveals our heart's capacity

to awaken into love.

Sam Oliver

Sam Oliver

Personal Notes

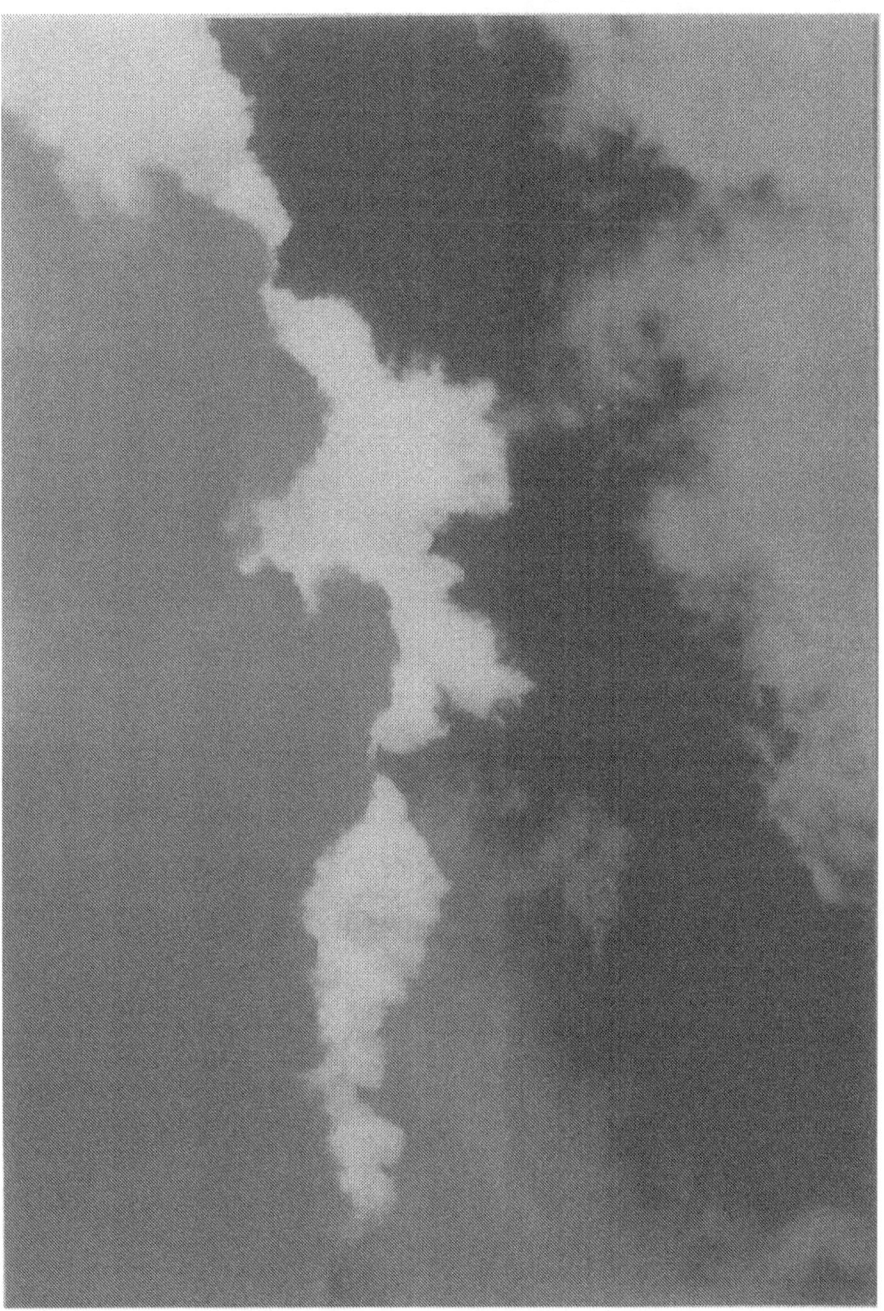

Integrating the Feminine Spirit

The love of a mother caring for her child is constant. There is nothing her child can or cannot do to stop this from happening. A mother is a womb for eternity to breathe into and create an awareness that eventually takes physical form. This awareness begins to identify with its new surroundings and feels the warmth of a loving feminine spirit surrounding him/her. Here, a child is bathed in feminine love approximately nine months. After being anointed inside the womb of its mother, a child is born.

Once a child is born, the need for a mother's love does not end. It is a time when the feminine spirit of a mother holds, feeds, and nurtures a child gaining a sense of personal identity in the world. Until this child was born, it was a child of the universe. Although a child's essence is bathed in eternal love, a child is born into human flesh. Because of this, a child's identity is altered and expanded. It is a time when the feminine spirit integrates a child into humanity.

During this time of integration, a child begins to realize what it has become. A child begins to notice it has the appearance of fingers and toes. These objects begin to wiggle, and a child begins to identify with these objects. Before long, a child is reminded that these fingers and toes are its own.

Attachment to these objects as one's own being starts the separation of total unity with the cosmos to a sense of being divided. At this point, a child begins to notice that he or she is both divine and human. This dance between the divine and the human aspects of our being becomes our path toward integration of the feminine spirit.

At this point, the love of a mother will not be enough to sustain a child in this world. This world has a way of confusing us all. The world tends to form attachments with our awareness pulling us further apart from our initial awareness before birth.

Like a gentle flower opening at the rays of the sun in spring. Our heart, our mind, and our soul are awakened at our center by "Mother Nature." Mother Nature reminds us that the core of our being is purity and love. As we connect with the "Divine Feminine," we return to the womb of creation. When we return to the womb of creation, we return to the same love that gave us life. In this sense, we are "all" children of the divine feminine of the cosmos. Yes, we are all "ONE."

Here, our human experience is filled with grace. We are given a sacred opportunity to express a unique aspect of creation no one has, is, or ever will again. We are blessed to have this moment surrounded by eternity. And, the instant we realize who we are as children integrating the divine feminine into our world, we are as gentle as a dove. We hold in our eyes, in our hands, and in our hearts what appears to be a distant memory. The memory of what brought these hands, eyes, and hearts into being. Yet, the divine feminine is more than a memory, she is the very one who sustains us when our body begins to experience pain and suffering. She is the one who helps us to enjoy love. She is the one who gives us hope to carry on when all hope appears to be gone. She reminds us that we are more than our appearances. She reminds us that we are children of the cosmos. Every encounter, every moment, every day becomes an expression of our awareness seeking manifestation into our world from the infinite depths of love as deep as a Mother's heart.

Inside each of us, there is a softness about us growing with age. As we mature, our gentle spirit has a strong desire to surface. It is the voice of the feminine spirit calling us home. This faint awareness awakens us to multidimensional thinking. Our multidimensional thinking opens our heart to feel on cosmic levels; rather than, a linear level alone. As our heart opens, soul is revealed.

The moment we shift from linear thinking to multidimensional awareness, a sense of unity takes shape. And, our mind, our heart, and our soul become one. Spirit breathes wholeness upon us. We are held in grace, in mercy, and in love. Our identity no longer becomes defined by externals. Instead, our identity is embraced by creative intelligence greater than our self. In this state of awareness, what cannot be seen becomes more real for us than what can be seen.

When insight "to see within" grows, we are integrating the feminine spirit. As this happens, we remember we are eternal and constantly held in this "stillness" behind all vibrations or sensations in the physical world. This stillness has been called many things. Each definition cannot describe such peace we all long for. This stillness is the womb of creation having the capacity to birth anything we desire. It is the feminine spirit of a loving presence creating countless expressions of creativity, streams flowing into countless rivers, and the awakened consciousness of that which lives.

Humans are very conscious of their consciousness. This gift moves us to protect our forests, help endangered species, and bring to life the heart beat of a child. As co-creators with this unseen force giving us life, we stand in awe of what is around us. In soul, we are reminded that we are always standing in the midst of a creation that once did not exist. In essence, we are always in the womb of creation awaiting the next experience of consciousness to appear before our eyes. And, when it appears, we will have come face to face with the heart of Creation.

Inside every human being (male and female) are masculine and feminine qualities. The masculine side of us projects forward what he wants to obtain. He is the linear part of us focusing his attention toward reaching a particular goal. He has the tendency to divide all that gets in his way and conquer his mission.

The feminine side of us draws in the divided parts of herself and the world around her to nurture, love, and heal. It is her

57

nature to care for what has been injured and broken. Our feminine side engages our heart in ways the masculine cannot. For instance, the masculine's way of engaging the heart is found in the statement "follow your bliss." When interpreted by the masculine spirit, we tend to think this is making our way in the world. It is somehow outside us to obtain. The feminine side of us reminds us that within us lies our essential nature and "the bliss" we are seeking outside us.

Our world stands at a crossroads. As we enter the 21st century, we are being challenged to integrate the feminine side of us. In the year 2,000, we now have more than 50% of our population being 50 years old and older. This has never happened in our history. This shift will cause us to reflect on how we are going to care for an aging population.

Our present circumstances require us to look beyond our own desires and intentions to create a kingdom of heaven for ourselves. We are challenged to recognize that the kingdom of heaven and its abundant living will be measured by the level of peace we experience within. Thus, the key to abundant living in the 21st century will lie in our ability to connect with each other on this level and share the unlimited manifestations springing forth from these qualities of relationships. These qualities of relating enable us to share our lives with each other on the level of soul. It is an eternal bond which has, is, and will continue to move us into the feminine spirit.

Integrating the Feminine Spirit

Inside us...

is an exquisite reservoir

of nurturing qualities

sustaining us.

Each dimension...

is filled with opportunities

and abilities to fulfill

our lives.

Our life...

is the manifestation of

our intentions and desires to

be known.

They are...

aspects of our life

tenderly cradled by

the feminine spirit.

Sam Oliver

Personal Notes

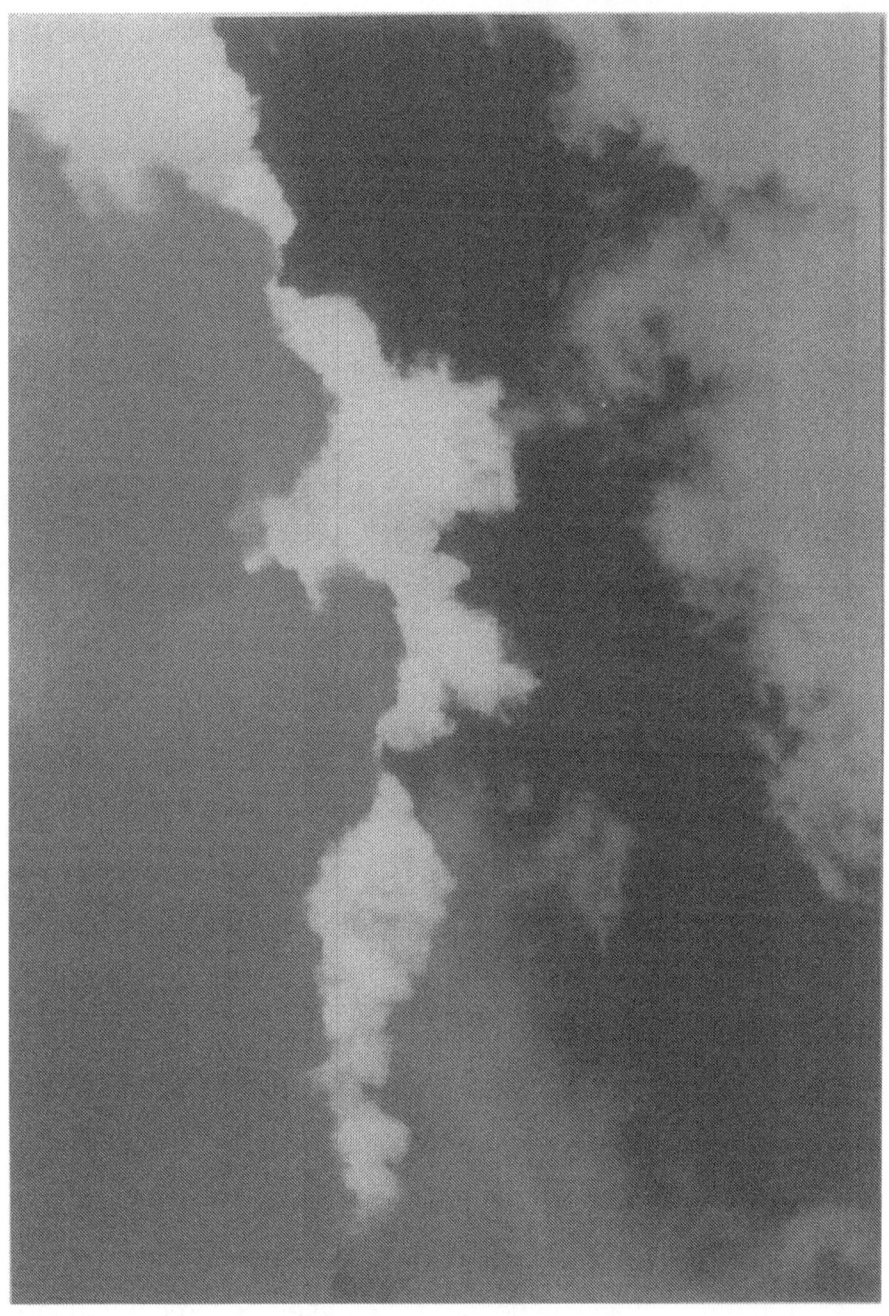

Returning to the Womb of Creation

Every night, we go to bed and close our eyes. As we close our eyes to the exterior visions of our day, we open our heart and soul to inner visions. We open our inner eye to the dream state. In this state of our being, we connect with insight. Insights are inner visions of our soul manifesting themselves through symbols in our dreams giving us cues to what is going on with us or direction for our future. They can be our way of retrieving our soul from the past, viewing these experiences, and integrating them with a spirit of love and compassion.

When our consciousness moves deeper and deeper into sleep, there are multiple layers of restfulness and turmoil along the way. Each layer contains levels of intense energy in our life that constitutes a collective awareness residing within us. As we move further into them, we enter into a very still spacial quality in our consciousness. This stillness is free from the layers of consciousness in the exterior and interior parts of us demanding our attention. We are totally free of distractions in this core of our being. In the stillness, we are bathed in the womb of creation. The womb of creation is pure and healing. It is a return to the innocent state, of which, we are all a part.

A few years ago, I was meditating. As I entered deeper and deeper into my consciousness, I saw myself becoming younger and younger. I became a youth, a child, an infant, and an embryo. I rested my consciousness in the womb of my mother.

I felt warmth, stillness, and sustaining love. I was being prepared for birth.

Then, I felt a tug at my awareness leading me deeper. I moved through the womb of my mother to the womb of my creation before my birth. In this awareness, I was no longer physical form. I was aware of my awareness. I had no beginning or end. I was connected to the universe in all directions. I had entered the boundless state. I felt electrified. My awareness, having no particular identity, traveled effortlessly into the sky, through the galaxy, the stars, and finally pausing to look upon a great light. My awareness returned home to my true nature. The identity of Sam was no longer important. What became my focus was remaining in this great light of peace and love.

My awareness slowly entered this tunnel of light guiding me gently into its center. I felt warm, loved, and blessed. I was totally centered in infinite possibilities waiting for my soul to embrace who I am. I became very aware of my capacity to co-create a life with the unconditional love of my Creator. I was home.

Hidden behind all the appearances of our lives are infinite choices. Within each choice is a choice maker. This choice maker is our essence. It is our capacity to purposefully move between the appearances in our lives. This spacial quality is our peace, our power, and our womb of creation.

Throughout our lives, we are given one opportunity after another to view our world through fresh eyes. Each day, we are given many ways to view our world through the eyes of spirit. Through the eyes of spirit, we are no longer looking at our world with simple sight. Instead, we utilize simple sight to focus our attention on people and circumstances with the eyes of soul.

In one lifetime, we will meet many people. Each person will give us an opportunity to view the world through their eyes. Each perspective will have different qualities of attention and intention. These qualities are seeds waiting to take root in those who have the desire to see them grow. Ultimately, we are ideas in the mind of God (Creator). We are implantations of spirit capable of fulfilling the ideal purpose of our Creator's will to find wholeness.

There is more going on in our lives than what appears on the surface. In the eyes of soul, we view our lives with unconditional love. This unconditional love enables us to live with the conditions we find ourselves. Thus, we are able to experience each event as a quality of existence surrounded by the gift of grace.

As we let go of our personal identity of our perceived self, we merge with what has no beginning or ending. We surrender into the womb of creation, whereby, what we return to is an identification with an aspect of awareness that is infinite. Here, we are eternal.

The movement into soul is similar to a caterpillar weaving its cocoon around its physical form protecting it for a rebirth. A caterpillar is aware of physical changes taking place inside it. It doesn't know what is about to happen, but it enters into a womb like state in order to rise from it a butterfly.

So it is in our lives, we are constantly entering into circumstances and events that will forever change us. Each experience expands our awareness in ways that alter who we are. Much like water floating down a stream. We are forever flowing down streams of consciousness. We can never step into the same stream or stream of consciousness twice. But, we can rest in the assurance that where we are going is not as important as, whom it is, we are following.

The feminine spirit creates unity out of diversity. She has the capacity to lead us into paths we had rather not travel. Each step of the way, we are guided and known as a child of the cosmos forever living the life we have been given. Thus, we enter into a dimension of our self that eventually leaves the self behind, in order to enter an experience of living not made with human hands.

Returning to the Womb of Creation

Curving back within oneself

are multi-levels of consciousness

containing unique expressions of living

revealing the nature of soul.

Each layer

unfolds various vibrations

releasing numerous experiences

of one's heart, mind, and soul.

As these experiences fade,

they are enveloped

by a mysterious presence

drawn from within.

It is the return of one's soul

through space and time

unleashing the womb of creation

where our spirit waits to be born.

Sam Oliver

Personal Notes

Closing Remarks

In every person's life, there is an inherent need to feel as though we belong to a much greater purpose than our individual needs and interests. As we shift our attention from personal desires to connecting with a power greater than ourselves, we feel a drawing energy pulling us from within. This pulling from within is sometimes referred to as a tugging of our heart. Our heart is moved to connect with an act of service that will take us out of our own ambitions and ego to serve the needs of others. Once this part of us is engaged, our heart becomes synchronized with the pulse of creation. We begin to view the world around us with a sense of compassion. We begin to care for our world as though it is part of us. As we go deeper into these patterns, we realize what we see outside ourselves is also inside us at some level. It will be a more symbolic revelation than literal.

This knowledge makes us very powerful beings. Within it, we have the power to heal or destroy. It is our mission to find what motivates us. It is our purpose to discover who we really are. As we place our gifts in areas of our world that has need of them, we bring peace to a situation, experience, and event.

Once our desire to be integrated into caring for others and our world as though we are part of it, we begin to merge with what brought us to earth. We are led to do a work, practice, or share a common journey. Invisible bonds hold us together with particular communities and become a binding force of energy reaching into infinity. They are the unseen force of our nature longing to be cared for. We all belong to this unseen force of nature. Here, our caring for each other penetrates our mind and emotions. We are caring for each other's soul.

One's particular awareness of the world around him/her has perceptions and feelings. When our mind sinks into our heart, insight is activated. As we look within through our imagination to make sense of what we see in our world, we move into soul. At this point, we look through our eyes instead of with them. Our world becomes an opportunity to create our world out of soul. Each breath, each action, each experience is a transformational vortex, whereby, we give a sense of meaning to every situation from our soul.

The deeper we engage ourselves in this way of living, the more we will view the world from the eyes of our feminine spirit. A mother cares for her children no matter what they say or do. Her children always remain in her heart. Even when a mother's child turns against her for a season, she holds them close with her love that connected them at birth. This birth was determined by eternity. It is a circle of love that cannot end.

Our hearts will not rest until we become one with the cycles of nature that join us. These cycles are eternal. When we experience these cycles with gratitude, we become aligned to spirit. As our soul returns to this center, we realize that our world does not belong to us. We belong to the world. The deeper we enter this reflective observation, the more we realize that our real Mother is not born of flesh and blood. Instead, our real Mother is beyond birth and death. She is spirit.

Our true nature belongs to Mother nature. She is the womb of all creation. She is the womb, from which, we came and, to which, we will return. When we return to this love, eternity opens our heart to a love that never ends. Here, our feminine spirit is integrated through the womb of creation. When we understand this journey, we become co-creators with the Cosmos. And, the dance between "Mother Earth" and "Father Sky" become a dance of our souls weaving the tapestry of our lives into the world we live.

One Sunday morning, I was walking along the St. Joseph River in South Bend, IN. As I looked into the river, I saw bubbles forming themselves in groups. These bubbles were being formed by a nearby waterfall just up the stream. Inside us, we have streams of consciousness shaped and reshaped by the world around us. Just like the bubbles, our thoughts create an awareness, and we are drawn toward certain groups or states of consciousness.

No matter what state we are in mentally, emotionally, or soulfully, we are always able to find a place in this world that will care for us, know us, and love us. There are times when we identify with being in a waterfall and our whole world has been turned upside down. Then, there are those times when we are drawn toward one soul group over another and merge with it like bubbles floating down a stream.

There are numerous bubbles (states of consciousness) flowing down endless streams (streams of awareness). Underneath them all, we will find mother earth (a foundation). We cannot see this foundation in the deepest parts of a river, but we know she is there. This foundation sustains us through our most trying circumstances. We are constantly held in her power. Like a baby held in the arms of a loving mother, our soul is held in the womb of creation infused by the power of the feminine spirit. As we return to this quality of existence pervading all conscious life, we are returning to the power of our Creator.

It has been an honor to write on the feminine spirit. It has drawn out aspects of my consciousness that has filled me with peace. Truly, life is a choice to be happy or sad. In the end, no one is to blame for our circumstances. Our circumstances reveal qualities within us needed to be seen outside us and integrated in positive ways. And thus, we need to take total responsibility for our lives.

We are each endowed with the love of the feminine spirit. It is my hope that those who read this book will use it to reflect on this part of us needed in our time.

Contained within the heart of every man, woman, boy, or girl is this gentle quality reminding us we are loved. May the Creator of us all bless each person who reads this book.

Sam Oliver

Epilogue

Dr. JoAnn M. Burke

(St. Mary's College of Notre Dame, IN)

The early years of the 21st Century have brought corporate scandals, a stock-market crash, terrorism, and war. State governments have been in a budget crisis and education, health, and social service programs have been cut. It seems that we have become quite disconnected from one another as our social responsibility appears to be diminishing. At the same time, courses in spirituality have begun to appear in the curricula of medical, nursing, psychology, and social work schools. Moreover, feminist, black, liberation, and post-modern thought have appeared widely in scholarly works. These approaches have offered new ways to view our individual and social situations.

Even though it seems as if we have become severely disconnected from one another, individual well-being cannot be separated from social well-being because we are very interdependent. The feminine spirit is concerned with this well-being because we are very interdependent. The feminine spirit is concerned with this well-being and interconnectedness. The feminine spirit has always been with us and continues to be with us even though it has been repressed by centuries of patriarchy. Nevertheless, this repression has not annihilated it.

Sam Oliver

Sam Oliver speaks of the growth of insight, the fusion of spirit, and the return of soul. Perhaps children are more aware of the feminine spirit than adults because our patriarchal socialization processes for adulthood neglect to value being and interconnection as much as doing and agency. Yet as adults experience the limitations of doing caused by the inability to control and avoid loss and pain, they may become more aware of the feminine spirit that exists deeply within the self and in the caring actions of others.

Changing the socialization processes for adulthood to include a higher value for the feminine could vastly change the behavior of adults. While a higher value on the feminine would be helpful across the life span, it is a vital need now with growing numbers of elders. More of us are living longer than ever before, and we do not know how to manage this situation. With the bonus decades of our lives, we have more functional years in the elder period of adulthood; however, elders move out of the "productive" work force, and we have been socialized to devalue periods of our lives in which we may be doing less. All of us, and elders in particular, may need assistance in learning how to turn our attention solely from doing toward being.

When we focus more on being, we turn inward, reflect upon our lives, re-work and release past injuries and pain, become more aware of our gratitude, and invest in the well-being of ourselves, others, and future generations. The world's wisdom traditions point us toward this process. Throughout our lives, this process is the feminine spirit calling us to the Source of all being. This process requires us to stop our frantic activity, to stop doing and become more aware of being.

While important for elders, this process is not confined to the elder years of adulthood. It is with us across time. Sam Oliver describes some of the experiences of this process in childhood and in adulthood. In more traditional terms, this book is about the human journey to remain connected to the heart of God - a God with feminine as well as masculine images.

Appendix: Exercises for Integrating the Feminine Spirit

Hold an Infant

The act of holding an infant is an opportunity for us to connect with our own inner child. Notice how people's demeanor softens in this act of holding a child. Literally, our hearts are melting. We let go of our roles as mother, father, friend, counselor, etc., and enter an empathetic state. In this empathetic state, two hearts become one. When two hearts become one, we get in touch with what infused our lives together. Our souls begin to unite, and there is a sense of gratefulness.

Play with a Child

To engage in play with a child is to activate the imagination. Children see our world as it truly is. We live in a recreational universe. The thoughts and desires of our heart illuminate our imagination. At this level of awareness, we move through the material world to connect with our soul.

Although our soul cannot be seen with physical eyes, our inner vision sees it clearly. Children are always at play with this unseen force within them. They use it to play with their toys, with their friends, with their imaginary friends, and with their parents. A child touches our hearts in ways seldom known in adult relationships.

As we engage in this kind of play with children, our souls are free. Here, everything is possible. There are no limitations. All is well.

Bake Cookies with Children

Children enjoy making things. They especially like baking cookies. Or, shall I say they like eating what they bake more. Does it really matter? Again, what matters is what is not matter. It is the heart felt connection between children and adults that moves our attention into the sacredness of this act.

Care for a Dying Patient

As we focus our attention on the needs of a dying patient, our heart begins to connect with the person we are caring for. We become empathetic to their needs and our attention centers on serving the needs of someone outside our own needs. This moves us from our ego and into the act of service.

Play a Game - Any Game

When we play a game, the act shifts something inside us. We become childlike. We leave behind our adult roles and responsibilites to play. At this point, we move from our personalities to our soul. We are connected to the Cosmos. We are in touch with the energies and feelings of being joy and peace. It is a similar feeling of being engaged with our mother in play at home or the playground. We are surrounded by the feeling of nurture that touches our heart and soul.

Hearing the Feminine Spirit

Sit quietly in a room or outside. Settle your breath, thoughts, and emotions. Feel your heart beat. Listen inside your body/mind for a gentle and soft voice. It is softer than your inner dialogue constantly talking to you. This voice simply notices life. It is directional and without judgement. She is a wise old guide teaching us to trust our hearts. Listening with our hearts, we will hear it leading us down paths that are fulfilling and full of peace. Her voice will not get louder with age, she will simply become clearer to us as we enter deeper into her love.

About the Photographer

The photos in this book and the front cover are the courtesy of M. C. Ward and Colleen Ward. Colleen began taking pictures when she found out that she had an incurable cancer.

M. C. Ward requests that any reprints of his wife's photography go through him. I want to encourage you to look closely at the pictures in this book. Some say that they see angels and many other images. Have fun.

A Final Note

Integrating the Feminine Spirit: Returning to the Womb of Creation is a model for healing through the feminine side of the soul. The purpose of this book is to outline a process whereby a person can understand and acquaint him or herself with an aspect of our awareness often neglected in our world today. Much of the emphasis in our world is on what a person can achieve without regard to how these achievements effect the world and the people living in these achievements. *Integrating the Feminine Spirit* is an attempt to give acknowledgment to the inner qualities of living that our outer world thrives upon us.

Just think for a moment what a child does and says when he/she gets hurt. They want their mommy. Why is it that when we are hurt that we look to the feminine soul for strength and direction. On September 11, 2001, the first thing we did when New York City was bombed was to turn inside ourselves in prayer, for direction, and for hope beyond our external world being destroyed around us.

This inward look into a world that is with us throughout our life is a womb like state of being. Inside us is an incredible source of strength and energy capable of nurturing a dying person through death, help us rebuild what is destroyed in our external world, and transform the most drastic event into a presence of peace. Thus is the world of the feminine spirit.

About the Author

Samuel Lee Oliver is a Spiritual Counselor at The Center for Hospice and Palliative Care in South Bend, IN, and Chair of the Hospice Ethics Committee. He also serves as the State Continuing Educational Chair for the Association of Professional Chaplains. Sam is an editorial review board member for the *American Journal of Hospice and Palliative Care, Journal of Terminal Oncology,* and *Healing Ministry Journal.* He has written numerous articles for national journals dealing with death and dying, and the author of <u>What the Dying Teach Us: Lessons on Living</u> published by Haworth Press, Inc. And, Sam Oliver is an award winning poet.

He began teaching and speaking about providing spiritual care more than ten years ago and continues to keynote and speak at public engagements on the national and international levels. Sam received his certificate in Healthcare Ethics through Rush University. Rev. Samuel Lee Oliver offers talks on Spiritual Care of the Dying, End of Life Ethical Decisions, and now, talks on the feminine spirit and how we heal through the feminine side of the soul.

www.ingramcontent.com/pod-product-compliance
Lightning Source LLC
Chambersburg PA
CBHW030341290526
45785CB00004B/1563